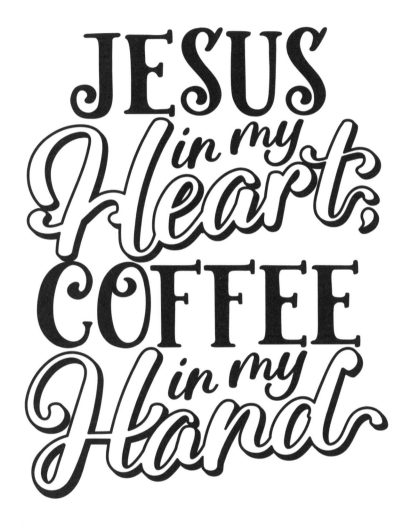

JESUS in my Heart, COFFEE in my Hand

CASTLE POINT BOOKS

NEW YORK

JESUS IN MY HEART, COFFEE IN MY HANDS.
Copyright © 2023 by St. Martin's Press.
All rights reserved. Printed in Canada.
For information, address St. Martin's Publishing Group,
120 Broadway, New York, NY 10271.

www.castlepointbooks.com

The Castle Point Books trademark is owned by Castle Point Publishing, LLC.
Castle Point books are published and distributed by St. Martin's Publishing Group.

ISBN 978-1-250-28556-0

Cover art by Kimma Parish
Design by Joanna Williams

Images used under license from Shutterstock.com

Our books may be purchased in bulk for promotional, educational, or
business use. Please contact your local bookseller or the Macmillan Corporate
and Premium Sales Department at 1-800-221-7945, extension 5442, or by email
at MacmillanSpecialMarkets@macmillan.com.

First Edition: 2023

10 9 8 7 6 5 4 3 2 1

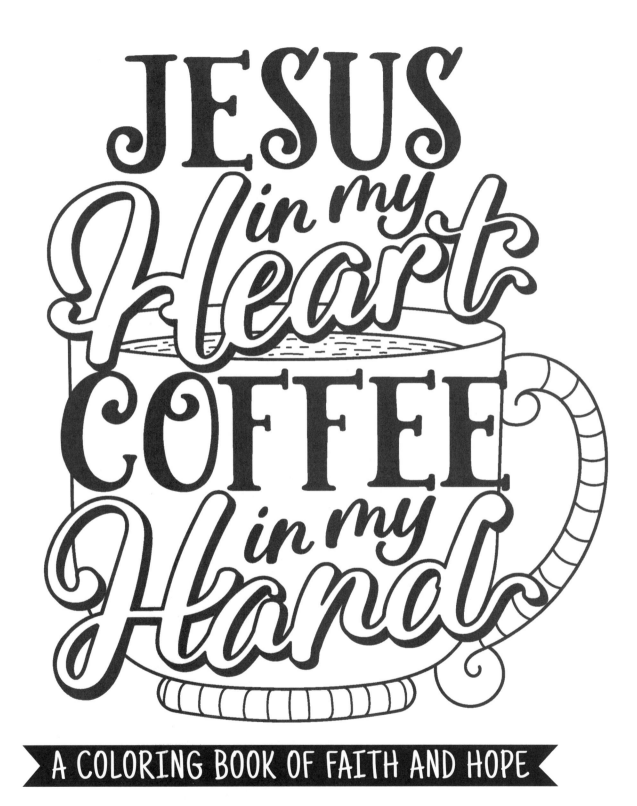

JESUS in my Heart COFFEE in my Hand

A COLORING BOOK OF FAITH AND HOPE

· HANNAH GOODING ·

I'm only talking to Jesus today

Bless my mess

(especially the kitchen)

LORD, SERVE ME UP YOUR FULL STRENGTH

FULLY alive
(UNLIKE MY HOUSEPLANTS)

John 10:10

Where two or three
are gathered, I'll be
with the dog

JESUS TOUCHED
MY WATER

This close
to flippin'
tables

DREAMSCROLLING ON ZILLOW UNTIL MY FATHER MOVES ME IN

John 14:2-3

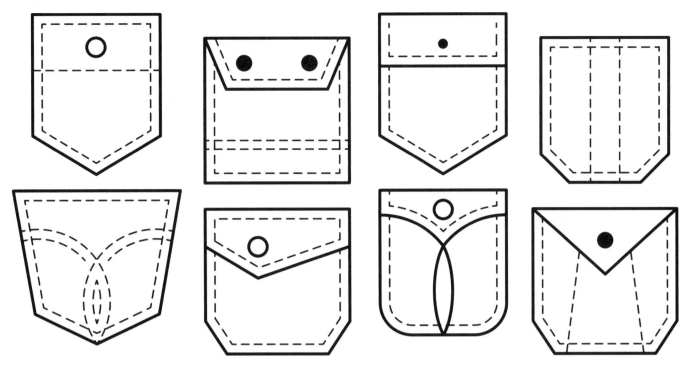

Waiting on a miracle
from Jesus

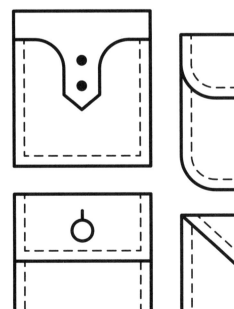
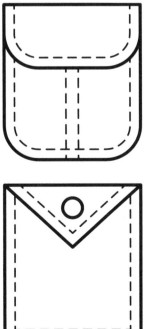
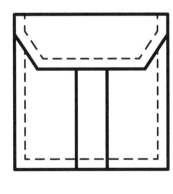

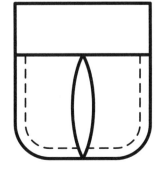

Sundays are for naps and Jesus

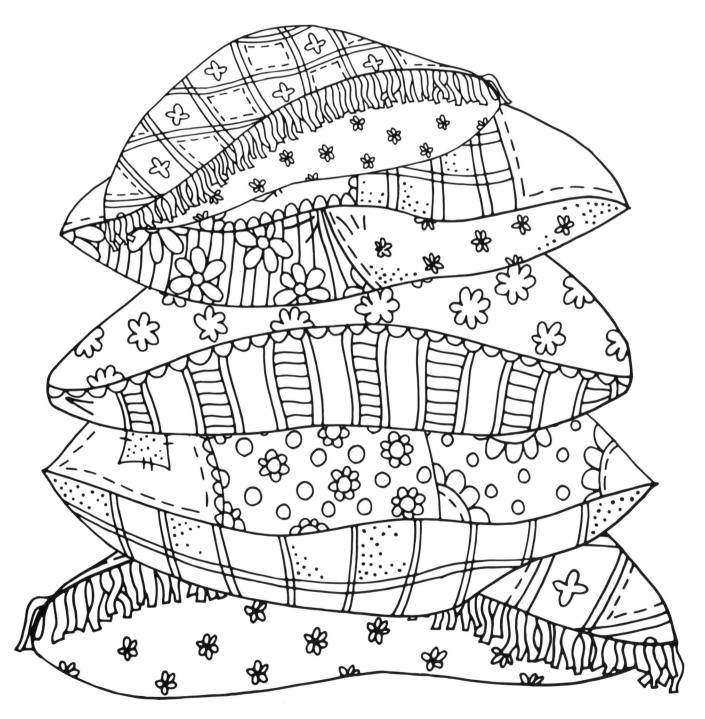

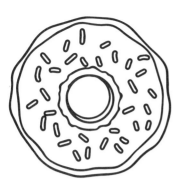
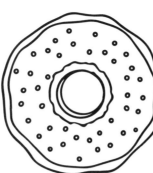
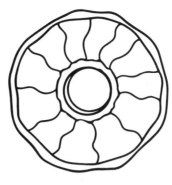

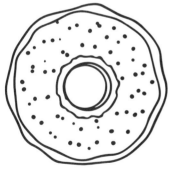
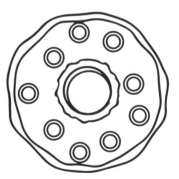

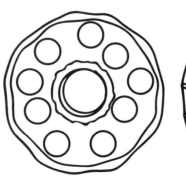
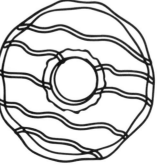

GOD'S WORD: SWEET AND FILLING WITHOUT THE CARBS

Psalm 119:103

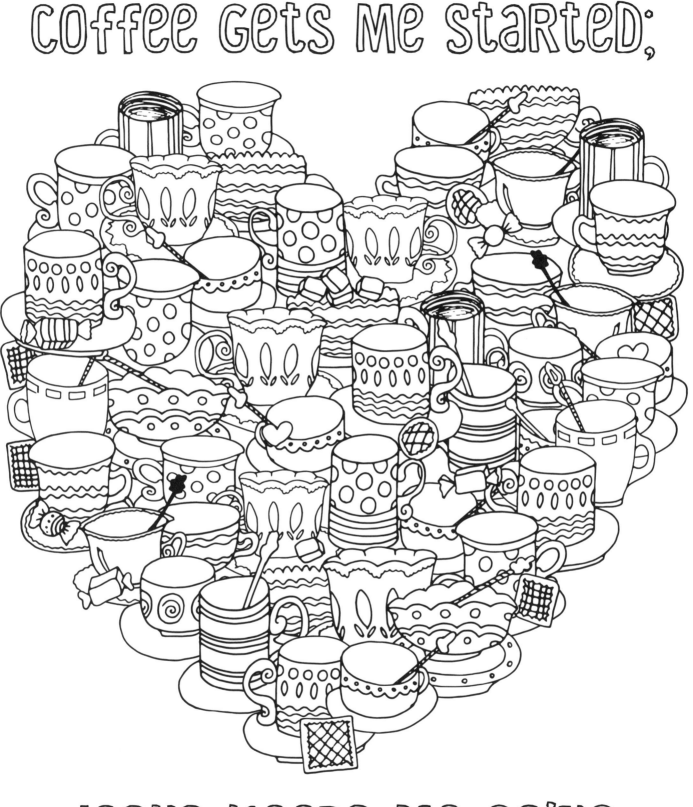

COFFEE GETS ME STARTED;

JESUS KEEPS ME GOING

Understanding why Noah only let animals on the boat

NO GREATER LOVE THAN TO LAY DOWN

ONE'S TRUE CRIME DRAMA FOR ONE'S BIBLE STUDY

If I'm going to be the feet of Jesus, I need some cute sandals

AND A WEIGHTED BLANKET

some days, i'm clothed
with strength and dignity;
others, i'm ditching
my bra the minute
i hit the mudroom

Tell me it's an answered prayer—
not about my car's extended warranty

Holy Spirit, you are welcome here ...

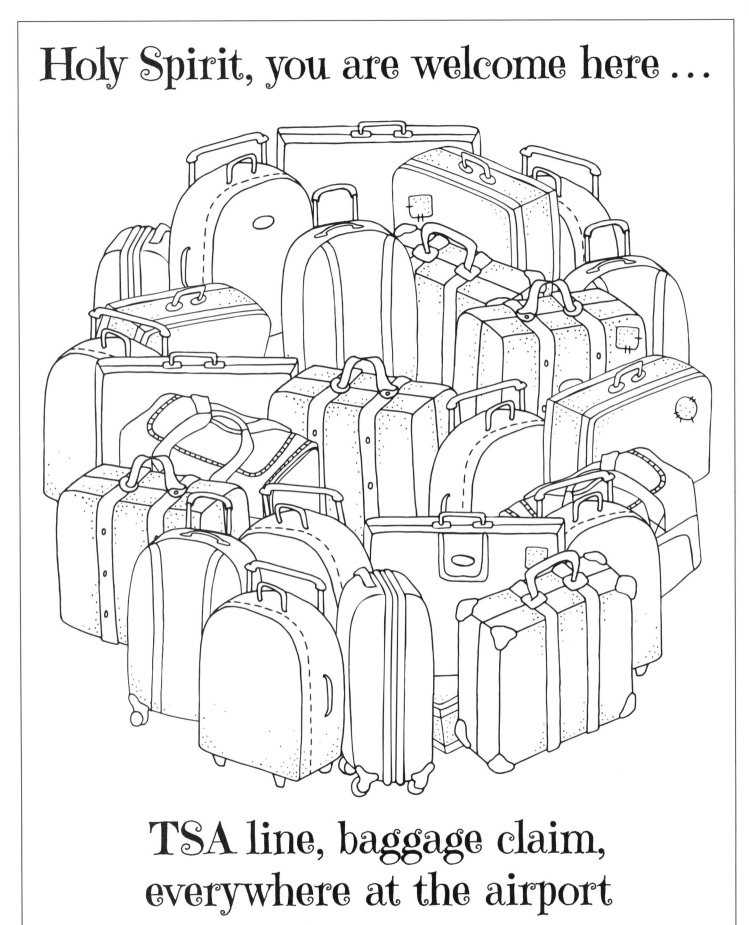

TSA line, baggage claim, everywhere at the airport

In need of a little refreshment to

get through the day's wilderness

2 Samuel 16:2

JESUS, CAN THIS BE MY
LONELY PLACE?

Luke 5:15-16

Wash me clean, Lord
(You may need a laundry booster after this week)

I will fear no evil
as I retrieve my devotional

BREATHING IN THE BREATH OF LIFE I NEED TO START THE DAY

Genesis 2:7

I wish FRUIT were my temptation

By wisdom a modern
farmhouse is built

Proverbs 24:3

Not by my strength but His

(with a little caffeine)

Philippians 4:13

Time for pumpkin spice yet?

Ecclesiastes 3:1